Nature Child

*The Journey Continues... Step Forward,
and Let Faith Open the Window*

Roxanne R. Mead

WestBow Press books may be ordered through booksellers or by contacting:

WestBow Press
A Division of Thomas Nelson & Zondervan
1663 Liberty Drive
Bloomington, IN 47403
www.westbowpress.com
844-714-3454

ISBN: 979-8-3850-1642-6 (sc)
ISBN: 979-8-3850-1643-3 (hc)
ISBN: 979-8-3850-1651-8 (e)

Library of Congress Control Number: 2024900598

Print information available on the last page.

WestBow Press rev. date: 02/01/2024

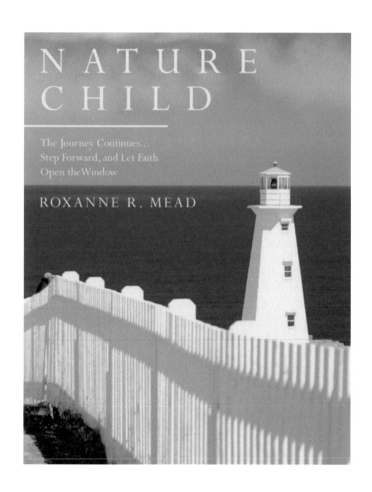

NATURE
CHILD

The Journey Continues...
Step Forward, and Let Faith
Open the Window

ROXANNE R. MEAD

"You are the light of the world."
—Matt 5:14 (NIV)

Contents

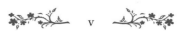

Introduction:

My doors of opportunity open in banking and finance. It was very fascinating to see the exchange of money from one penny to millions, but I wanted to learn more.

And when the doors opened for me in a corporate operations position in a large information system, and technology, I was ready to be a part of a fresh start up team learning telecommunications. This at the time was the third wave that later became the fastest growing movement of its time and the most fascinating of all.

I learned you had to ride with the tide of change because the only thing that was not going to change was change.

The management kept telling me I needed a degree if I wanted a high grade level promotion. It was not very popular for women to have leadership positions; however, I was determined that I wasn't just an ordinary woman.

Trusting my father, I asked for his blessing, and I went to college earning my bachelor's and master's degrees. No one in our family had done that, it was quite an accomplishment.

Funny what was unique about this was having these degrees I still needed to be every practical. Reality it was only a dream piece of paper in a big world with so many changes in my field. I somehow was going to utilize this training to enhance my skills and experience. This goal would enable me to have a better lifestyle.

I wanted to do more than just pay household expenses. I wanted to make an impact on this world. Questions entered my mind, yet I did not really know how to start. I just wanted to and acquire ideas to create a plan for my future reality.

From my parents I learned just do it attitude, you will have to work for anything you want. Their words echo in my mind "and don't do it halfway give it your best."

Now if you learned a little about me by now you would know, I could never be satisfied with just showing up.

I desired the approval of the senior management team and knew I could do this job. They had a good reason to hire me, and I was going to honor their mission statement and values that they believed in.

Because I was giving my life each day to what they required I saw this as corporate marriage both sides had their responsibility to having a successful vision fulfilled.

Truly I did enjoy what I did, however our economy was tested nationwide. Again, we were all faced with having to focus on our future and the next change.

Perhaps being an August baby, "Zodiac Leo "was more to me than I recognize, and I liked glamour and good things. This factor caused me to stretch more. I was going to walk on water and learn a new field as a skin care specialist and marketing cosmetics total glamour. Now if you want to be the best, then you will have to go and learn from the best. I decided I wanted to learn from the European French firms such as Guerlain, Christian Dior, Lancôme, and Channel just to name few.

Now who does not want to be beautiful, all genders desire beauty. I could not settle for less than give it all I had to be a part of this circle of friends.

Time does not stop and so facing the truth I had to ask myself this question? What was I going to do with the rest of my life?

I looked at what I did right and what I could do better.

Taking and reflecting on my vast experience, I checked my resources, and said it appears we need to make a new plan.

Now I knew this plan was going to make a major change in my lifestyle. I was going to awaken my dream with a book to enrich and awaken the hearts of people to respect their talents and learned skills. They would value themselves and learn self-respect. This would be like silk thread that could be woven and blended into a tapestry that would evolve from their experiences in their journey of life.

I knew that a people must first want to desire to make a change. The fact is that they will do what is best for them. Also, to really desire to make this world better, we will all have to participate as a team because this cannot be done by one single person.

As I was reflecting on my life, I saw the little girl sitting on the steps of the back porch writing enjoying the breeze. I remember she loved the fresh air as she wrote in her journal the little birds sang their song. It was there she decided to give herself a secret pen name "Nature Child".

No one would know it was her, the little girl who loved walking barefoot on the cool green grass and picking small violet bouquets. She would sing with the birds chipping as she walked in the sunshine.

Happiness to her was writing for in her heart she knew one day this dream would become a reality. Her purpose was to be a writer, known as the-author called to offer inspiration to all. Now it was her secret buried but one day it would become real.

If we choose to see the unseen through our eyes of faith in God, we will walk down the road of our destiny. Mine was Nature Child's Journey

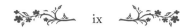

Nature Child's Journey

Nature child, come take my hand. I welcome you to walk with me and together, we will walk on the shores line water's edge of the sea. We will watch the tossing waves dance in the sun as they play and have a lot of fun. I have given them this strength and gentleness too. Yes, this is true, and I made them able to bow down just to honor you.

Let's enjoy the warmth of the fun that I'll place on your hair. Smell my fresh clear morning air, as it blows over all your cares. This sun was made to offer you light and to warm both morning and night.

The stars I made them too, and they also were made to govern you. Take this time and rest in me for I am the one who made all of these. Great are the works of my hands and far more than mankind can understand.

Now let us ride with the wind, and the clouds will take us over many mountains to take a closer look. Do hold on tight to me for my wind will be more than a gentle breeze. Look, there is where I grow my beautiful blue heather. You will learn that its roots are strong, yet the flowers are as light as a feather. Today, my gift is my awesome weather.

Yes, I know you love the warm sunshine with its nice breeze. Now my cool springs move through my valley and waters the trees. Notice the river that travels across my meadows and into the streams this awaken many of mankind's dreams.

That's what my desire is for you to live the dream and purpose that I have made just for you. Trust in me is all I ask of you, and now I'll show you what you'll need to do. Lay all your burdens down and allow me to restore your crown. For you, my child, are very precious to me and a part of my royal family.

When you are facing many challenges in life as we all do, they make you think they're closing in on you. Stop, and allow me to show you ways of letting go of all that heaviness feelings.

A simple resolution to regain your peace is easier than you think. Here is some good news that won't cost you anything known as a "Nature therapy". See yourself just stopping long enough to breathe in the fresh air. You have chosen to take a walk for fifteen minutes outside.

Listen to the little songbird, see flowers tossing in the wind. Now place your cares on the bottom of your shoes and walk over your worries. It may sound

silly however it works. Stepping forward confirms you're going to walk out your solution. Hope is restored and your heaviness is lifted.

Inside each one of us there is a hidden treasure map that will reveal your talents and the purpose for your life. Note there is not any form of partiality given to anyone as we are all created equal and very valuable. You are a Masterpiece, now hide these words this in your heart and remember to respect who you are.

On the Tide

Early one morning before the dawn, I went walking as I felt torn. I was on a journey to find me, and I always found comfort when I went walking by the sea.

The wind was blowing softly tossing my hair when I looked down and saw a small starfish lying there. Washed in by the waves facedown, I saw a few air bubbles rise from the ground.

I felt that I needed to extend my hand and do something for it was trapped in the sand. The starfish was trying to make its way back into the sea even after the cruel harsh storm had broken the beautiful star fish form.

Wanting to help, I reached to save it from being harmed. As I held it in my hand, it spoke to me so gently that I could barely hear or understand the plea.

The small voice said, "Toss me into the sea. I want to feel like I belong to the sea from which I was born. I was rejected because I just didn't fit in. My body wasn't strong enough to swim, and the strong currents of the wind broke my fin." I truly did understand as I too wanted to feel accepted and to feel like I belonged.

The starfish wanted to find its worth, so I asked what I could do. "I'm desiring to swim home she replied". "You've done all you needed to when you picked me up and gave me a chance, so I will be able to dance once more. Across the top of the waves, I'll swim home once again, leaving my stardust in the wind."

Holding her for a minute longer, I touched her gently and said, "I believe in you and I'm going to walk out into the sea and find the best wave then set you free. Don't be afraid of the challenges you'll face for always remember my gentle embrace."

The little starfish seemed to beam from within as the dawn's light fell from the sky and wiped the tears from both our eyes. It warmed my heart to see her swim, knowing the odds she took with that dive, yet I knew she would survive because her confidence was stronger than the tide.

In our lives, you will face hardship and rejection. You'll face sorrow and pain even if you've done nothing wrong. These challenges create the real you and a true gold tried in a fire that will guide your soul. Then you'll discover the real powerful and beautiful you. Remember I believe in you.

Dust and Gold

I walked into this dark musky room and what did I find, but a worn-out mahogany table broken lying face down on the ground. I continued to explore and found several pieces more. This wood was of good quality; however, it just

looked like it was left behind. Now it's say "One man's trash is another man's treasure" I thought to myself.

Dust and dirt were everywhere and in everything I found. It looked so sad to see such despair. And yet I said, there's got to be hope, so I pulled out the little chair. I tried to open the drawer, and the small knob was loose falling to the floor. Was this a sign saying to choose now if to stand strong and not to turn and hit the door? I wanted to walk away. It was not my job to clean this mess. I had to wonder was this just some kind of a challenge test?

A small voice spoke these words that to this day I won't forget. "I once stood in high honor with royalty, you see, and they knew me across the world and on the open seas. My dress bottle was designed of the finest crystal and pure refined gold laced my throat. My final touch was my seal that locked my fragrance top with a gold designed-like lace that makes a crown glistened around my throat. And to this day, a lady treasures my crystal bottle and will not just toss it away, knowing my heritage dated back through centuries as fragrance worn every day."

Startled being caught by surprise I asked, "Who are you?"

She gently replied, my name is "Shalimar." My mystic fragrance of bergamot, Iris, and vanilla notes made me famous throughout Europe and the world for centuries. Her bottle sparkled in my hand, she was very proud of what she did across our land.

I now better understood my purpose, and I needed to create a plan. I was to restore what had been stolen from this lady that once stood so grand.

Where would I start, only God himself did know. But with his grace and wisdom, they would know that they saw beauty replacing ashes and a legend from long ago.

When things have been taken from us because of our chances its hard to cope with it. We don't like that we're out of control. Change will occur, so we must

adjust and refocus on what we will need to do next. Don't let yourself be caught in a pity party to long, we must take courage and move forward with grace to embrace our new journey ahead.

Take the good you learned offering this simple prior experience you had to help someone in need, this hope is the light in life today.

Against Wind

The wind was tossing my hair as I watched the storm bring in a force of power that threatened the air. Large dark clouds rolled across the sky. Then and one right I saw the flash of lightning in the distance and felt the warm and cool air clashing as if they spoke a dare.

I was feeling restless, almost anxious, for I knew this was a sign that spoke to me as if it was written for all to see, craved in time waiting for me. The sky was soon going to send her rain. For some unknown reason this brought tears to my eyes I couldn't explain. Why did you bring so much pain?

Small little birds swirled and rushed looking to hide, they seemed to know the powerful force of danger was in the air as the leaves tossed here and there. Now part of me wanted to run for safety. I felt like something was trying to make me afraid. This was a fascinating storm and I'd felt powerless as the wind became threatening this early morn.

Lightning hit an old oak tree and took one of the branches down that fell close to me. The new leaves from recent spring were being challenged to give in and surrender to the wind. Now the older tree stood strong knowing that he needed the rain even if it meant that he could lose his form. The wind howled as if annoyed as she saw this tree as just her toy.

I knew I had to decide to remain or to make a run for the shelter from the rain that stared. Now inside my heart, I knew there was something here I needed to learn so I stood holding firm. I had chosen not to be afraid as I wanted to be a part of this mysterious thrill.

It was like the stage was set for this event with me as mankind, animals, and nature—we were all there. Now in this circle of life, who would really be in control?

The calling of an eagle was in the air, strong with a voice that seemed so nearby. I looked up through the clouds, high I could see him there. Then he broke through the storm with his wings spread across the sky reviving his power no one could deny.

Now not against the wind but with it he flew. He embraced the challenge and dared the lightning to strike him too, he proven his skill would outwit the storm for he knew his power and how he was formed. He called out to the wind "just do it" and he did.

His strength was amazing as was his power. A feather from his wings fell softly into my hand. And I reached out to him sending a message with words unspoken yet he did understand. I said, "you don't need to be afraid of this storm for this was why you were formed. Just remember who made the storm and you're the symbol to be adorned for our Nation and around the world too. You're in the message of freedom printed in the colors "Red, White and Blue ". It is known we'll need to stand strong if our Nation is to keep her liberty and the honor from which she was formed."

You will be challenged to fear different experiences in your lifetime. Know that in you is the power to embrace fear. And when you do, we'll see the strength in you that was given as God did not place the fear in you but rather the power, love, and a sound mind.

Break These Chains

Experiencing this pain, I felt that I could not be denied, today my pride rose its head and tried to fill me with dread. I had to experience the truth that the one I had loved and trusted had been unfaithful. He had lied to me and was filled with a raiding anger. I had to pull myself together or I would always be trapped in a prison of self-inflicted pain. I feared I would do something I would regret.

This wound had cut deep, and I cried how could this be happening to me, I thought I was smarter then to let my emotions rule over me. I can't no I must not let this be the end of me.

An echoing haunt of the past filled my mind, saying what a fool I was to have fallen for this false deceitful affection that exposed my need for love and my vanity.

He had wanted fantasies without honor living in a world of double standards. I would have had to live a lie to enjoy the care and sharing of his offered affection. His heart was only selfish. He spoke with hidden lustful desires. I believed him because I trusted him and thought this was love.

I had the right to hate him. At least to blame him for hurting me. Wild as they seemed these words confused and rattled my brain; Gods hope once remembered rose from within my heart and echoed with in all my parts. Was I to be just a reflection of what I had believed? Or only play like I'd never read His words. This lesson was a test I said. I'll walk through the fired to prove I'd believed Him.

A quiet voice spoke in my ear said lay down your fear and cry out to me, tell me about this awful deed and what you need because I am always concerned about you and want you so talk to me. I will heal your broken heart but you must do your part. You are given free will to do as you please, so now it's time to speak to me. I'm here to restore your soul and make you whole.

One's choice will be given to you, if you let this hurt rule your soul this vengeance is like fool's gold. You can choose to believe and trust in me, and I'll give you the grace and mercy to set you free. Or you will be a hostage in chains with hurtful anger and its pain tearing at your brain. Know that it will destroy the good in your heart as unforgiveness stops me from helping you. Now tell me my child what do you have to gain? It's your future that lies ahead, let go of this misery and receive this grace instead. Then your life will have the joy that your need. Together we will enjoy eternity.

Life's Broken Pieces

Looking back at my life what did I see but so many broken pieces are all a part of me. It's said beauty for ashes could be given to me. It would be easy if I'd only lay down my pride and believe than God's grace would be given, and these chains would be released from me.

I wanted to turn the bad to good, so I gave it all I had and left behind the old neighborhood.

Now in some ways it looked a lot better, and it looked like I'd come out ahead, but the pain was still in my heart and with the feelings of emptiness and dread.

I couldn't stop the memories that flooded my mind of being so betrayed and trust that I could never find.

As years passed by I learned that I was not alone, for many had come through the same path feeling empty and no place to call home.

I see there is much misery in this world and many things that made us sad. You would hear "I'm not a bad person I just wanted a little fun ", maybe someone would love me and I'd would meet that special soul someone.

Yes, it seemed it was a small thing to ask and never to be found for many lives have been taken because their treasure was never found. If you looked across the globe you'll find it everywhere people without a purpose and in such despair.

It wasn't meant to be this way from what I understand a price was paid for everyone and it's still true today. Hope and joy could easily be found if we lay down the lies that's have been spoken and crush the evil under our feet. Let's talk about how peace on this earth could be found, with one small hug offered to the person stand next to you that would say I do care about you.

Faith would open the doors to believe there is a purpose for each and everyone. Our efforts could mend this broken world and all this pain would end. We will stop all selfishness if we reach out to each other, and all become friends. It'll take courage and strength to look within and not pretend. We'll have to be honest with ourselves, if not there will be a price in the end.

From the beginning we were given a choice to have life or death. Now how will we spend the rest of our life. It will start with the decision we make today. Our weakness will become our strength, if only we will ask for help and grace.

Being strong is not the muscles in one's arms nor the strength in your legs but it's being honest from your heart and looking at the mistakes that you've made.

I can't make you do anything, it's really a personal issue of choice. Everyone is equally qualified to decide. I pray you're choose to value yourself and life.

Dawning Light

I laid down but found a little rest knowing in few short hours I would be put to the test. Would I live out the remaining of my years or see it end with just a few small tears? War was raging in my soul. All I wanted was to be whole. Fear raised its ugly head making it hard to even breathe recalling the diagnosis that revealed the virus Covid-19. Heavy my heart did beat as I laid in my clean linen sheets.

I'd dreaded making this decision after what I had read, yet I had to do something or soon be dead.

No one could take the breath from me but only the one who spoke life into me. Like the dawning of a bright sunny morn, strength rose from my heart and these words were formed.

I'm not under the curse of sickness and disease, and it will take more than this to take the life from me. Is it not written that he said, "Believe, I'm willing to give you the desire of your heart and set you free." Mark 11:23-24" NAS

All I had to do was trust Him and believe He is the one who wrote my destiny. The journey which lays ahead, holds a future of hope that will be mine as I choose Jesus Christ to be Lord of my life and into eternity.

We will need to be accountable and responsible for our own issues in life. Having free will we choose how the cards of life are dealt to us. If you don't make your own decisions as to what's best for you, you will have to accept the decisions someone else will make. We don't need to blame others. It's time to make your choice. I hope you'll choose life that will bear good fruit for your labor.

Taking Time

What was I really made of and what did I truly believe? Sitting back, I took a moment just to breathe. The day was coming to its close as the evening sunset was just beginning to fade.

Her clouds were beautiful and perfectly adorned. Dressed in colors soft and warm. Who doesn't treasure a moment like this when you stand quiet and take in all this? Enjoying the sun rays that danced and twirled in the sky, as they quietly floated by.

The Master Artist was at work from what I could see, creating colors as far and wide just for me. Simple yet such a treasure to behold as I reflected on the memories, I now do hold.

This was my present on this beautiful day. I will always treasure it for it meant more to me than silver or gold. What I saw was breathing awesomely takingly and so dear to my soul. I pray one day I will ride on those clouds to the streets of gold. There the true glory will be there to behold.

I shared with you my love and laughter and together we experienced what really matters we cared. This is life.

Bubbling Brook

Beside this beautiful bubbling brook, I stopped and took a closer look. The water was refreshing, so cool, and clean, dancing in the sun leaving rainbows that glistened in this lovely stream.

With her diamond shoes, she danced for me, creating small twining lights that bounced back at me. Smiling at the sunset as she was just about to go down when I found myself wanting to lie on the ground just to be still and look around.

The wind blew gently with the sun still warm as I watched the water swirled and turned. As a child, I had heard this tune that the stones sang as they gurgled soft bubbles with the lune.

She asked, "Where is the child in you that loved to sing and play each day as she then giggles and go on her way?"

The reflection in the water I saw was me, and I had to wonder just what did happen to that little girl in me? Just who was this adult grown up person looking back at me?

We are all so busy being busy with the cares in life. Have you ever stopped and said a quick hello to someone passing by but never really let them share how they really were? I believe that we've all done this. Start now today, be still and listen to that neighbor, co-worker, or perhaps it's your love ones. I promise that it will be worth it.

A Small Velvet Box

I found this small little box that someone had thrown away. It was velvet with a satin bow that had signs of age fading with wrinkles as I ran my finger across it. I knew this treasure was going to be my little place for all my thoughts I wrote and secretly hid them under cover of this satin lace.

Now as the days pass, I found the time and used it wisely. My thoughts were full of hope and joy, it was a sense of freedom when the words went across the page.

This gave me encouragement keeping each phrase.

Today I wanted to share what was in the box and so I took it to be seen. The old schoolteacher said this is your box of gold. Inside your dream is hidden, it needs to be seen. The world is standing by waiting patiently and they need to be told.

I offered her one of the writings and I turned and walked away never thinking that it would win such favors that those who read them would want more. I had never been recognized for even a single thing and now these little writings meant everything.

They offered me a scholarship to a school that would teach me how to do what I had planned. I couldn't speak with the words of joy that seemed to be caught in my throat. Imagine that someone cared enough to offer me a fresh brand-new start.

All I needed was permission to go to this fine school so that I could be someone special. My writing would be called a tool. It would open the door to my tomorrow and all that I had hidden inside.

Now all I needed was a yes, for a dream that couldn't be denied. Several years later this box was never opened, as it was crushed with one blow as a voice echo that said no. I'm not allowing you to go. Who are you to think you're anything you're not better than me and you'll never be anything, tell me why you'd do such a silly thing.

With tears in my eyes, I touched the box once more and then set the box to flames so no one else would make me feel such shame.

I felt she told me the truth and I could trust what she said after all it was my mother and the one who offered me my first breath. Facing reality, this dream was only a fairy tale to me.

I could only hear the echoes of how worthless I was and never be anything. I was only foolish thinking about past and that had to end.

I couldn't run from the pain that was engraved in my soul. This hurt had done more harm than any beating that I had taken from her. All I wanted was a chance to try and be the writer who offers hope to all the world. They could read my stories and receive hope, and perhaps a moment of joy.

I buried my writings thinking they would never be seen again. People say as you grow older, you're supposed to be wiser. It was time to sweep the cobwebs from my mind. Only l could remove the devils' dagger from my heart. I decided it

was time to let go of the rejection, self-pity, and my pride.

I learned not everyone wants you to succeed. They selfishly only want what's in it for me because of their jealousy and their greed. Wisdom taught me not to play their game even when you wanted to have the fame you needed more to keep your Integrity.

If we offer love somehow it will make its way back to you. Trust me, character is formed in the fires of life. I believe the truth is something we all need, and no one will ever take it away from you. Today make the choice to walk forward unafraid knowing if we look up, we will see a rainbow shining in the clouds saying you're stronger than you think I am with you in the storm.

Grace helped me see how to embrace my Journey. Yes, fear did look me right in the face. However, fear is only false evidence that appears real. The true power in you is greater than what's in this world.

Pain and love are on the same road. Mankind is the highest form of creation; we all need water and air. Each of us has been given a special talent and a purpose for our fulfillment.

Don't let someone or thing steal this from you.

You need to be a part of making this world complete. I don't want to just survive. And I want you to live life and enjoy the good of each day. Now what's your choice?

Twinkle Little Star

You're twinkling at me brightly tonight, little stars, though you're shining at me from afar. I know you see me down here; it's true. I have a question that I would like to ask of you. God gave you the job to watch over me by night and to offer your bright starlight. Did you happen to see my mom passed through your sky last night? As she was on her way to heaven, I thought she may have passed you by.

For in a twinkling of a moment, she was taken away though I had hoped things wouldn't end this way. I wanted for her to stay with us that's why I prayed. I don't have the power to stop what I knew was true. She was gone, and there was nothing I could do. I really didn't have a clue.

Standing close to her grave, I placed a small rose next to her name engraved. I knew I could not save her from her pain. My offering was an outstretched small hand that felt so helpless, yet we had believed she would walk her journeys and then pass through the gates of heaven and meet her friends.

The tears filled my eyes as only one thought entered my head. I would have to bear the truth that she was dead. My world at this moment was shattered, twinkling star. Don't you see I wanted to say this wasn't happening to me. I'm always so strong and know what to do. I couldn't stop the shattering of my heart, I felt I was falling apart.

I cried all the harder and shouted out to God, "It's all your fault that you took her away. You took my mother to an early grave. You said you loved me, and this is what you've done. You wanted me to trust you and to believe your word was true. You said you work all things for the good. Was there something I misunderstood?"

Another voice whispered in my ear, "Deny Him, this was never true He isn't even real." Hurt and angry, I felt confused, yet I knew somehow these words had to be true. Many times, I had seen with childlike faith that I could say yes I believe in Him.

"Lord," I cried, please take away from my heart this pain for it's more than I can embrace. You know I just lost my father only eight weeks ago and now my mother too. How could you be so cruel? The man who said he would love me forever has walked away when I needed him the most. He had nothing to say.

Call me for I'm deep within, now I heard these words, "*I am* the one. I am here now drawn from me. Your strength you need as we'll walk through the valley of the shadow of death. I'll be with you. Questioning, "What does that mean?" I wanted to scream.

Through the tears, I thought I felt Him reaching out to me, and it was now His tears that I felt on my cheek. I said I am so confused, was this really God or my wild imagination?

Then I heard, "I will not remove this pain from you. You must bear it, but I will bear it with you. I will not forsake you, and you are not alone for *I am* with you always. You are not alone."

Truly no one understands the pain of grief even if they have experienced the loss of someone special themselves. Each time it happens it's different. Only with grace can you process this part of life.

These words are now burned into the core of my soul, and it's in them that I was able to take hold of His strength as I have lost seven members of my family.

His Dream

This was just a flask of perfume that he held in his hand. Yet it was more to him than many would understand for in the bottle was his dream. Now he was going to the royal palace to offer it to the Asian Empire as a gift for their King and Queen. Many had scorned and mocked him saying, "You'll not amount to anything" as their hearts were filled with jealousy that he would do such a thing.

They shouted out to him, "You're a fool who'll only be seen as a joker by the royal queen. "Their words tore at his heart as he passed them in the street. If he believed what they said, it would mean his defeat.

Tears were in his eyes, yet he would not let them fall. No one knew what he'd been through to create his fragrance sealed in this small crystal ball. He chose to hold his tongue not speaking an unkind word. But he rather offered only a smile looking straight ahead for his dream could not be dampen as he walked on instead.

The legacy fragrance continued still today. Now ninety plus years have passed since that day, and this luxurious fragrance in her refined crystal bottle stands in the hall of fame as she paved the way to the open doors of fragrance and skincare that still stands strong today.

You will find this will happen to you too. Sometimes from those closest to you or perhaps total strangers who hear you wanting a better way of life. Your desire to success is so real that their unwillingness to step out and do the same leaves them threatened.

Pride and jealousy instead will show its face. Now this is your test. If you believe what you're doing is true enough, you will walk through scorn and embrace what it takes to have what you were born to be yours. And what you believe in now will become a reality. A future with hope starts today with faithful steps moving forward, walking over the rejections, lies, poverty and defeat.

Who Are You

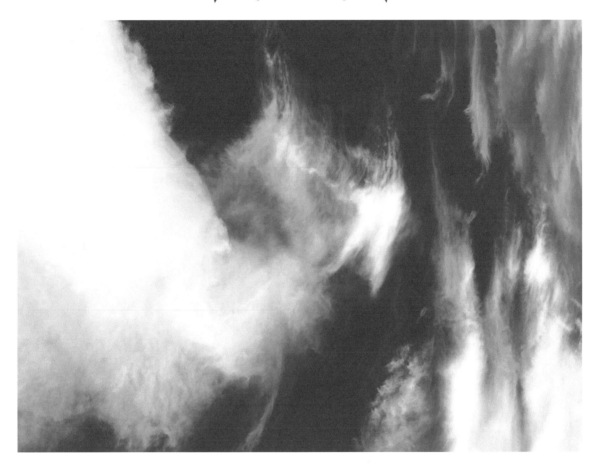

The questions you will want to ask yourself are simple ones. However, what makes them hard and perhaps difficult for you, is the way you see yourself. You may have net worth that's very impressive. Or self-worth that makes you feel you really a person that's got their act together or believe you do.

Are you sure you're being honest with yourself? Today may be the right time for a self-evaluation that reflects on facts not deceiving fantasies. We all are greatly influenced by those around us. Example, parent's, professionals you work with, teacher's and even social media. What we hear and see will also make its impact such as music, art, what we read regarding worldly issues in the news, and even TV programs.

Do you really want the true reality of who you really are? You're reviewing your assets verse's liabilities hoping to look good on the bottom line and come out ahead of the game.

Self-worth is a bit tougher and not as easy to make a proper assumption. Your age, gender, race, religion, culture and even time and events of your life are all facets of acquiring a filtering of what you may call truth. We usually believe and evaluate each day this information and our mind accepts these facts classifying them in various categories that you're willing to believe to be trustworthy as respected truth.

Be still for a moment of quiet .Yes, I'm serious I'm challenging you to be still long enough to think. Our world around us is filled with events that cause much confusion and fear. We question each day what reality is and what do we believe.

When was the last time you restfully slept a full six to eight hours or made a warm meal and sat down to eat it? Tired and hungry patients don't want to resolve even a small issue of conflict. Start today to value yourself. Be grateful for the water you drink and the air you breathe proves you're alive and have the present day to have fresh start.

Freedom is Your Choice

FREEDOM is your choice; you'll make it inside your heart, and it is transferred to your soul. You can only be the person that chooses to break the chains of locked in memories of yesterday, even today. This is what hold you back. If this is not done there won't be any peace of mind. Only you can open the door leading to a better lifestyle. Now with the truth you will discover what you need that will set you free.

This is force of interference what holds you back from fulfilling your dream. However: only you can take the steps forward embracing the unknown. You'll have to lay aside your fear even if your stomach threatens to turn your insides upside down.

The unknown is very much a challenge. We can't control the unknown. Yes, we are creatures that like control. Why, because it's our safety net. The person who's quiet and barely noticed is just as demanding control as the person who is loud and rude .

Now let's get back to embracing the things we are most not wanting to face head on. Again any person that does not want to confront chooses slips to the side of the room sitting in back of meeting feeling weak and powerless.

Their imagination runs wild, demons pop out of the walls flooding their mind with the worst thoughts that will happen to them.

What if you chose to cast your fears into the fire pit where they belong with the devil the author of lies. Now take back what really belongs to you your life and live it more abundantly. Take a fresh breath now, enjoy the truth that you are now entitled to freedom of what's held your back from your better life style.

Explore the possibilities available to you, others have created so many wonder things even when told they were not smart enough, the wrong color, too old, too fat, too skinny and not ever believing what your heard inside your own head when you looked in mirror.

There are people all around you that need what you have to offer, listen to their comments, respect their opinions, you don't have to agree with all they say however, you may add something to them they need. We need our family but what if there isn't a family to enjoy? Well, in this world there are a lot of people without a family. Don't rush into getting involved with the wrong people because you're alone.

Love takes a lifetime to be created. Time and patience to listen and learn about the person you're attracted to. They have a history and so do the ones that they associate with. This is an area of great concern. Thinking love will solve all is a fairy tale. It's work to make a marriage work. Caring more for your mate than yourself. Forgiving quickly or offered statement "I was wrong please forgive me." Use wisdom and knowledge to see the truth in what caused a problem. Resolution to the issue is easy when dealt with within a small window of time. Make a choice to be free of the burden by letting it go before it eats away at your soul and destroys you. "So, if the Son of God has set you free you are free indeed." John 8:36 NIV. Take back your peace and what belongs to you, your joy. You're not meant to carry the burden and worries that's God's job. He promised he would care for you, and he does not lie.

We don't know what we're doing or how to do it, we can't see into the future. Be Still get quiet and reflection on wants concerning you. If you rush in mistakes are made, and then worries set in, the failure and finally degrading of oneself or others. Yes, I've done my share of this. Time has cost me a lot of hard aches because

I'd did not think there was anyone who did care to help. I wasn't afraid to take a risk. I like adventure. But the walk would have been a lot smoother if I asked God and waited on the Lord. Ps 27:14 KJV "Wait on the Lord to renew your strength." EX 15:2 KVJ He knows all the detours in the road and how every one of them can be dealt with or avoided.

Everything that has life has time previously set in place. In our journey there are seasons for all things. A single seed planted takes time to create a rose brush and then the rose becomes a beauty bouquet you maybe must enjoy.

Burning Light

Stressed on every side, there's a private war going on inside. My heart is pounding—beats per minute (BPM) out of control. I'm trying hard just to keep hold for all that glisten is not gold if the story was rightly told.

I've tried to do what was right and yet this battle was more than one person could fight. How were we ever to win for we were all tired and just wanted it to end?

A burning light from deep within spoke. "Just breathe in. Take your strength from me, and I will take these burdens if you hand them over to me. "You were never meant to bear this battle alone for I paid the price before I ascended to my throne. "Now place your dreams and broken heart in my hand for I am the only one who can truly understand. I know what you have been through. And I have every teardrop that fell from you."

Did you not think I saw what they did to you for when they hurt you they hurt me too? Release this from your heart, and I will give you a fresh new start. You must take my love that I am offering you, so you will be able to forgive them too. For they know not what they do when they made a fool of you. This is my battle, and I will fight it for you.

Now hear these words of wisdom I am giving to you. I am in all you do, and there is no room for bitterness in you. Let my light shine forth like the dawn for in you, you'll find your song. And let the healing waters of life flow from within, and I'll restore your peace and joy. Amen."

Hope is needed that will be like fuel to a fire. It's what helps us to press forward in life. What benefited value is it to you to hold on to the wrong doings that were done to you. Is it worth that sleepless night? It's your stomach that tosses and turns. God fights that battle. *"For vengeance is mine, I will repay" saith the Lord.* Romans 12:19 He will help you forgive. Let's go! step forward be brave and courageous.

Taken Hostage By Pride

J ust wanted to be perfect was the last words she had said. As the doctor turned and walked away these words were echoing in his head. Today they laid her in her marble stone coffin cold and pronounced dead. Her life was filled with much turmoil, and despair there wasn't any chance of hope in her mind.

They said no one was with her that would have stopped what had happened when she needed them the most there was only the empty house with its ghost.

From the outside they only saw a very beautiful lady who dressed in style. A woman who had enjoyed satin and lace all laying in place. She would enter a room and somehow you knew there was someone special in this place.

They spoke of her highly and thought they knew her well. Yet she had fooled them all, for she never shared her fears and anguish of the vision she was locked in a darkened cell.

Not even once did she let down the glass wall that would have revealed it all. This is where she hid her memories that taunted her by day and caused her to slowly fade away.

Trembling, she laid in her bed. Tormented by her fears she did not dare to tell. This was her misery that she bore, and it just was not fare who would care that this was really how she dwell.

Wanting to scream out "they were cruel and crushed my heart. She had allowed them to destroy the last hope of having her dream".

Oh, how she wanted to be happy and have joy each day. Perhaps if she wasn't so weak in her faith, things might of went a better way. And she whispered these words gently as she faced her demon that was tormenting her today.

Wanting to know what love was, for it was only words on a page that seemed never to be found. She was always disappointment that seemed to hang around. Today she had lost the treasure that was greater than gold and the price was she sold her soul.

There wasn't any peace to be found for her worries has stolen it away. Feeling more frighten and defeated she tried just to make it go away. Again, the voice

in her head screamed "who do you think you are you'll never be anything, don't you see how worthless you are."

Recalling the memories of these spoken words when she was just a child, it was this that had opened the doors allowing the darkness of rejection, fear, and pride. There was no mercy nor any place to hide as they now attacked her from every side.

She wanted to climb out of this slinking hole. If she was only smarter, or wiser she would have known what to do.

Feeling weak and helpless she was not able to fight back.

The weight of this was greater and she was afraid to act.

Her fear caused her to feel weaker than before as the tears touched her cheeks, she just couldn't handle this and did not want to fight this battle anymore.

If there was someone she could trust. Someone she could talk to, anyone who would stop long enough to show that they cared. She wanted and needed answers to her questions and to stop all she feared. One hour of their time would have helped perhaps given her a clue as to what to do.

Soon her life would be over even now she was short of breath. Trying to take one more step and keep up her head. The wind chilled her with illusion that brought back such dread she believed she was worthless this was the lie that caused this beauty's death.

Many have been in these shoes and don't know what to do. Are you going to wait until it's too late and then they'll only read your name on your grave stone plate? We have a choice. Wisdom learns from the mistakes, what you did right and what you could do better.

Pain will play a part too, let go of what hurt you. Now the truth is though the grace of God you can be healed of what caused your hurt. And yes, help you to

let go of the pain. You'll find you can forgive, and you'll want to live. He wants to heal your soul and then you'll be whole and able to truly let go.

You may think that your all alone however the "Spirit of God "is right there with you, He's not too busy to answer your prayers for help.

If you are trying to do it all on your own your pride won't allow this to be a reality. It's not wrong to want to be accepted, you need love and directions for your life. Its time you realize you weren't meant to have all the answers.

Gods the one who takes our imperfectness and turned it to perfect. His grace and love flowing with the Spirit of God "The Holy Spirit "your comforter and guide.

Just for the record you're not big enough to be God. Go ahead and laugh its good for your soul. "A merry heart does good like medicine. "Proverbs 17:22 NKJ

You're the one who must make your decisions for your life. Others make comments and have opinions. You don't have to believe what they say is the truth. Play smarter not harder I believe and have confidence in you that you will have faith in yourself. You deserve to have a better life without being bitter.

We have the right to freedom of speech but that doesn't give us the right to tear down someone else's charter. A simple act of kindness does wonders to people of any age or color. Give a hug and don't be afraid to take one.

Be a Butterfly

Like a butterfly with brand-new wings who wants to fly high into big blue sky even if it means they could die, the destiny for each of us is set in place if we'll take the risk an embrace. The first step is hard to take to break the chains of fear and disgrace.

Reach out and stretch your wings. Be challenged, and yes, you'll see tears, yet you'll appreciate the love and happiness when it's offered to you for your happiness in life can only be found in what you choose to do. Do you have any talent you shall see for no one ever told you what you could be?

Many feels like having a dream is too hard to believe or even just conceive. In reality, no matter how rich or poor, we all have talent yet don't have a clue of what we are really called to do. Now if you'll be still, there is a small voice speaking to you. For it's said that we all have a purpose in life, and yet this isn't learned without a fight. Who would be keeping score if you were to succeed or hit the floor? Don't be afraid. You're really not alone for there is someone

watching over you from his throne. He knows already what he placed in you because he loves and does care for you.

Trust me. You are special. Look at your hand, each finger is needed, and there's only one set of your fingerprints. They can't be duplicated. So go ahead, be happy. It's okay to enjoy each day. Laughter is good. Merry heart does good like medicine.

Little Blue Bird

The air was cool and crisp this morning with patches of fog everywhere. From my window I watched as this little bird still in his nest welcoming the day and hoping for the best.

He's all alone sitting in that tree for a large hawk took his mother and the other three. He's not sure of how to fly. Now because he's so little I heard him say" it's just me with a few feathers on my wings". I'm trying to hide in this tree and I hope that hawk does not come back for me. I'm cold because of this morning's breeze yet I'm grateful I'm here so Ill sing and ill wait on the sun to thaw the spring.

I want to help this little bird however there's nothing I can do. I'm going to say a prayer and ask God to help him through. He's got to try to spread his wings and fly.

So he can enjoy what's natural has for him to do. So I looked out the door and spoke to this little bird, he must try and fly into this morning beautiful blue sky.

Who can help him he's so afraid? Now he isn't quite ready to fly but if he stays where he is he's surely died.

I see the pain and the fear that was in his eyes as he looks at me and said I really want to fly. In the cool air from the dew, he shivers and doesn't have a single clue.

As to where to start or what to do. Well it is as true he knew he must be strong and have courage too, if he was to fly.

Or just become easy prey for the hawk that would return to finish what he hadn't done the other day.

Bowing my head, I said a little prayer dear God, I know that you care and we need a miracle to help stop this despair. I know you can for wonderful are the works of your hands. I believe you can because you love all your creation and even man. Have mercy on this little bird you only need to speak the word.

The bird heard me for in the sky the sun was rising sending warm rays that offered hope to this little friend, his life was not going to end.

I know God will show the bird the way and He'll help him each day. A miracle happened in that tree, though I'm not sure of how it was done. Nor did it matter to me. All I know is this little bird had been given a chance to be set free as he spread his tiny wings into the sky with the help of the southerly wind, he was able to fly.

Now that day I really didn't know how it happened, yet it was true a little faith and belief gave this little bird a way to make his dream come true. He's tiny that know no one can deny, and I told him to be courageous and spread his wings don't look back just head into big blue sky.

I'm sure he'll face many challenges as we all do. However, I hope one day he'll return to my tree and bring back with his new family. I'll listen for his song for its nice to hear this in the air and know God did care as sun rays spread across the morning sky.

Truth is all creation is faced with hardship and joy in their journey of life. Today we choose to deal with things. Through our faith in God, we will have the wisdom of what to do. We need to know how to rest, for He knows what's best.

Perhaps you may not have liked that someone else had made wrong choices in your earlier life. However, we are responsible today to deal with this. All that has occurred has been left like dirty wash and you must deal with it. Now how we act, or what we say, your words become your reality tomorrow.

If we have integrity in our society a trust in God is key to making a better lifestyle. We are all valuable with gifts to share with others. As you give, it will come back to you in this journey. Your purpose for your life will be fulfilled.

My Special Copper Penny

Opening my back door as I often do, I wanted to enjoy the peace of the dawn and the view. A cool refreshing breeze was in the air that brushed my face and swirled my hair.

Sun rays stretched across the misty morn sending lights that beamed and formed a breath taking rainbow that sparkling in her rays, somehow it sent a message to everyone this was the beginning of brand new day as God's grace was showing us He made this just for you and me.

This was going to be a beautiful day with just few clouds that wanted to play. Warmed by the sun, I stepped outside. My shoes looked up saying, "Let's take a walk and see the wonders that were created for you and me."

Relaxing, I breathe in the fresh, cool, chilling wind. I couldn't help but feel refreshed and renewed as I felt blessed. Stretching out my arms, I tried to touch the sky. Who wouldn't be grateful for this awesome morn and all the wonders that only God had formed?

Cares wanted to steal this peace from me so I spoke in my heart, "Lord, keep me focused on the good I see." This is my present. I won't let it go for someone might need it that will pass my way, and I'll offer them hope instead of dismay.

Walking on sun rays sparkled in my eyes when I saw something that caught me eye. Twinkling back at me was a small cooper penny that spoke so softly to me, "Please pick me up in your hand."

Buried treasure, I chuckled, now mine to behold. Touching it gently, wiping off the rain and sand. Reviewing what was printed by man, it was the dated 1952. In God, we trust.

My heart leaped and warm tears filled my eyes. I couldn't even speak for this was the year that I was born. Somehow, a bond was formed as we had both weathered many storms, yet we are still as valuable as the day we were born.

Now this simple message I hope will help you too. You were meant to live in peace each day, so reach out to someone with a kind word and say, "In God, we trust to lead the way."

We never lose our value. Aging will happen. We must agree because mother nature's clock is ticking, oh my, dear me. Grumble we may, but it's so true. Ashes to ashes, you will return, so use your talents and value what you learned.

Queen of the Garden the Rose

Our lives can be seen in the rose for her stem is strengthen as she grows. Now if you would take a closer look, you'll see her beauty that fascinates both you and me. There is no fragrance greater than the rose for she is the queen of all that flowers that grow.

Now the rose was given a special purpose in life for her beauty would give life. Knowing this, she needed to be assured that she would be provided for.

So the leaves were created to guard the velvet petals as they grew. And the rose smiled because she knew the dream in her heart would soon come true for one day she would be a boutique just for you.

There are two parts of a story to make it true, so here it is the other side just for you.

Symbolic in her thorns is that in life there is scorn. Whether caused by vanity, failure, or shame, we all have to embrace the pain.

Now since the beginning of time, there is a facet of truth that we can't hide. We all will fall because of our pride.

It will be at this moment perhaps that you will stop and look at the blossom at the top of her stem and remember there is beauty to be seen in the end.

Now only God knows how to make you strong for from His nature you were formed. Knowing you need kindness and His grace, he has offered a sign for the whole human race.

With outstretched arms upon a tree, he paid the price for you and me. That was our sin and penalty. These same arms that were nailed to a cross, never to forget the cost of what it would take to set us free from all our guilt and misery.

Crafted like pure gold in fire is where true character and strength are formed. Now while there is still time, take a moment and embrace that you too will have to count the cost as to what you will gain and what will be lost.

Didn't the butterfly have to struggle to free herself from her cocoon? And didn't the chick have to break out from the egg to be your Sunday dinner? Well, yes,

we may not like it, but we were never promised a rose garden without the thorns. My hands have felt there pain, so have yours. But who doesn't like the fragrance of the rose.

Who's That Lady?

No one really knows from where she from as she was so basic and so very plain. From the ashes she arose, no one knew her from where she came or goes. She did not want any fame, but there was something special about her just the same. There wasn't a reason to prove anything, and yet there was a tugging at her soul. Not really knowing why, she just wanted to feel whole.

The choice was hers so I was told as she spoke to me saying, "I want to know before I'm too old just what was I supposed to do? Now I'm told that in my life there is a purpose just for me, so I can tell them I did it, and would never be filled with regret. I had filled my God given destiny. I know I have God's wisdom and I'm to trust Him to lead the way, following Him as He will know what's best for me. I'll succeed and accomplish this goal. Rather than never having had what was mine to behold.

Battlefield of Life

Nature Child is your offer to explore the use of Nature Therapy. The words in this book will offer enlightenment that gives your spirit peace that empowers and awakens the strength in you.

This nurturing helps heal the wounds that were made by the darkness of rejection.

You were once left feeling helpless and weak. It is time to awaken the truth within that gives you the light to receive the comfort and assurance you need. It also extends to you the power to take the strength that hope offers. You will now be able to overcome what was once meant to destroy you.

Take back the authority that was given to you. From the beginning of time, you were made to be the highest form of creation. It is your choice to choose to receive the love and acceptance that belongs to you. You have a right to live life more abundantly.

Only you will allow your mind to receive what you call the truth. You will conceive WHAT YOU believe and create your lifestyle by these every day.

What do you gain by thinking everything you have heard is the truth. Are you going to allow someone else's cruelty to be your reality? It was their pain and

weakness that you heard when they spoke to you. How ever it does not have to be yours to believe, it is only their opinion, and you do not have to agree with them. You may choose to agree or rather to not agree.

A good example of love is seen each day in nature as each season offers a fresh start with hope and new life. In your journey, your life is like a garden. I suggest you plant good seeds, water them and with good care you will see flowers grow.

Now remember it is your choice if you want your life fulfillment to prosper and have enjoyment.

Be a Butterfly Spreading Your Wings

Like a butterfly with brand-new wings who wants to fly high into a big blue sky even if it meant they could possibly die.

Somehow, we know our destiny for each of us is set in place. We only have to use our faith to embrace the mysteries of our heart. We will find ourselves wanting more, now if we just step forward and open the door. It is like a force that pulls from one's soul as they want to discover the key to unlock the answer to the question, what will make me whole?

And then the question we all ask ourselves, what was I meant to be? One greater than that, why was I born? Desiring to stop the empty feeling of misery that you do not belong you will have to choose to make the decision to open your door of the heart.

At first it is hard to take and break the chains of fear and disgrace. Reach out and stretch your wings. Be challenged, and yes, you will see tears, yet you will appreciate the love and happiness when it is offered to you for your happiness in life can only be found in what you choose to do.

Do you have any talent you shall see for no one ever told you what you could be?

Many feels having a dream is too hard to believe or even conceive. No matter how rich or poor, we all have talent we could use, yet we do not have a clue of what we are really called to do.

Now if you will still be, there is a small voice speaking to you. For it is said that we all have a purpose in life, and yet this is not learned without a fight. Who would be keeping score if you were to succeed or hit the floor? Do not be afraid. You are not alone for there is someone watching over you from His throne. He knows already what he placed in you because He loves and does care for you.

Trust me. You are special. Look at your hand, each finger is needed, and there is only one set of your fingerprints. They cannot be duplicated. So go ahead, be happy. It is okay to enjoy each day. Laughter is good. Merry heart does good like medicine.

Mystery in Mirror

I saw a vision of a man shaving, trying to look through a mirror that had fragments of broken glass.

He was afraid to touch the glass, for it would continue to shatter, so he struggled to see his face.

In the background a voice quietly spoke saying this was a reflection offering a vision of the broken pieces of his life. Now you are afraid to touch them because you know what will happen.

Truth is if you ever told someone how much they hurt you, you would not. It would be easier to hide these feelings. And just focus on what they think about you. You don't want your friends to believe your male character is weaken by feelings.

The voice spoke once again, "I'm right here and I have been waiting all along for you to say catch me I'm falling. You want rest and a small moment of peace. The price is high because your pride gets in the way. You're not wanting to admit this is greater than you are and that's frightening, you won't admit you're scared.

You can't control it, nor you cannot explain it, you just feel the emptiness.

In the past you heard there was a God, but is it a reality that He would care about one man's broken heart?

Again, with a gentle voice, this voice seems real but is this God? He said I'm right here, use your faith and trust me. I will heal and restore all the broken pieces and give you the care and love you've always wanted.

This is needed by many; however, they never know how to ask me.

Each soul cries out but few will try and find me. I'm right here waiting for you.

Jn14:27 NKJV "Peace I leave with you, my peace I give to you, not as the world gives. I give unto you. Let not your heart be troubled nor be afraid for I am with you always even until end of the age,"

Male and female alike we just human. We are very fragile just as glass that can be easily broken. In life we are not promised a rose garden. Now the graceful rose has many thorns, so has the journey of life. We all are asking in these last days where how to have peace that will quiet our minds. This is the question we live with each day in this world of harshness.

As a small child you may have been taught right from wrong. There was a price you paid for your disobedience. Who do you think taught your elders the golden rule on how to treat others? Wicked actions don't go unnoticed.

The rule to forgive is example, states we are to forgive those who have willingly wronged us. Why must we do this, you want to ask? because we will be robbed of our peace and health. Your heart can't hold bitterness and be healthy. The injustice will be dealt with in the final hour when we all stand and are accountable for their actions. Who do you know is willing to lay down their life and authority so you can have the grace to have this peace you need today? There is only one who has rocked this world from the beginning who knew we didn't stand chance without His love.

Natures Garden Reflection

Flowers here of many colors and shapes, make a beautiful display of nature. We are like this field many beautiful people one world to share it with simple truth.

Yes, seemed it was a small thing to ask and never to be found for many lives have been taken because their treasure was never found. If you looked across the globe, you'll find it everywhere people without a purpose and in such despair.

It wasn't meant to be this way from what I understand a price was paid for everyone and still is a fact today. Our joy and hope could be restored if only we lay down the lies that caused our pain. Simply the solution is just to stop this confusion and fear that peace will be found.

Faith would open the doors to believe there is a purpose for each and everyone. Our efforts could mend this broken world and all this evil would end.

We need to stop all the selfishness and try to reach out to offer to be someone's friend.

It'll take courage and strength to look within and not pretend we must be honest with ourselves, if not there will be a price in the end.

From the beginning we were given a choice to have life or death. Now how we will spend the rest of our life will start with the decision we make today. Our weakness will become our strength, if only will ask for help grace will show us the way.

Being strong is not the muscles in one's arms nor the strength in your legs but it's being honest from your heart and looking at the mistakes that you've made.

As a suggestion from a voice of caring, I can't make you do anything it's really a personal issue of choice. Everyone is equally qualified to decide. I pray you choose to value yourself and your life style.

MY SUGGESTING GUIDANCE FOR YOU TO CONSIDER WOULD BY CHOICE
The door to life is open and only you can choose to love or accept what life offers.

We must be both responsible and accountable in our lifetime. And you will find you will be rewarded with a blessing in your time of need.

So go ahead and reach out to help others. Here is my hug its free, so take one and give one. Happy nature trails to you. Step Forward as you cannot walk backwards.

Quiet Please, I'm Thinking

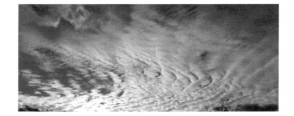

Fall is soon coming I can feel the cool crisp air freshening the room. Quietly I'm sitting allowing my mind to reflect, it's a miracle for me to just be still. I just wanted to rest for a moment. The window open blowing nice breeze across my face that leaves the message "relax" enjoy this gift of today.

I asked myself, what would happen if you had a chance to walk away from all this unsound thinking? I thought, "do you mean to start over" with a clean slate. No regrets, guilt about mistakes that I had made, nothing to fear, never again lonely. Maybe even enjoy some happiness.

I could have the next twenty-four hours to decide on making a change in my life. Questions flooded my mind about what I would choose to do differently. First, there would have to be a new plan filled with a purpose offering excitement. Next, I would need the wisdom to see the fulfillment for if I could see process leading into progress to enjoy its success. I would enjoy what I had accomplished.

I must respect my spirit, soul, and body. I'd never want to be overworked into the state of exhaustion. The right nourishment and exercise to refresh me would be a necessity. Watching never to destroying its metabolism with wrong beverages. Now, I can sleep peacefully and wake up refreshed at the start of each day.

This is not impossible it is more just a mindset of simple self-respect for the gift of myself and good health. Now, here is the biggest challenge to review," my soul" that can be a times my best friend or worst enemy. It will instruct me on what to do based on what I believe to be true.

Let's make this personal, "What do I believe" to be true? Who has influenced me and what steps I will need to take. What I do today is what is leading the way into my tomorrow. I can decide to sit still and do nothing, headed nowhere with no hope, the question then would be why would I believe I'd be happy and enjoy a better life?

Happiness is a gift felt in the heart. It was meant for us to have life and to live life more abundantly. God said so, He doesn't lie so we can trust Him. He created the earth with all its wonder and beauty.

If you have ever enjoyed walking at sunrise or experienced seeing the sun setting you were blessed by His awesome masterpiece seen in the sky. Today this is our nature therapy letting go of the stress around us.

It's easy to get too busy being busy I've done it, so have you. Is it time to take time, ask? what has stolen your peace. Today, I'm stopping to take back what is rightfully mine, my joy. And I'm sharing this with you because I care about your life. You deserve to be loved; we need each other to be whole. Look up into the sky see the smallest birds flock together form letter "V" victory they embrace the wind together. Let's learn from them. We all need hugs so here is one for you, now find someone and give one away.

Author Offers Words of Encouragements

No matter what race, what age, what education, or no education, we still need to fit in, to feel like we belong. This is making the invisible a reality. It's just to be loved and find peace. Today we need to reach out to each other and say, "I'm here. I care about you."

I challenge you to touch this world in your daily everyday walk because we need each other. We are not on this earth to just struggle through life and barely survive. You are special and one of a kind. Look at your fingerprints.

They're made just for you. They can't be duplicated. You are made marvelously whole and complete. Your future is bright, filled with joy, and the promise of better life. The choice is yours. You were given a free will. Take this gift of today. It's your present.

Now I hope you'll enjoy life's blessings found in each of us. It's a new day. However, what you've done with it is your choice. Always remember that there's someone who loves you and will always believe in you. Take this message even if you can't just truly understand it now. You'll have to trust faith. It's your open door for your hope of a better tomorrow. It's time you choose life and live more abundantly.

I believe in you. Always remember that and hide it in your heart. When the light is dim, hear these words and be encouraged. Cry if you need to. It's only human. We have feelings. Male and female—we are given a heart. I hope this book has planted good seed for your life. We all must choose to love or just accept.

My Wish for You Is This!

Open the door of your heart, and don't be afraid to dream. Now use your faith and believe in you. There you'll find the ability to see your dreams come true.

We all have a purpose in this life that's why we were created. When you do, you'll help make this world a better place. Today, know that I believe in you. Now it's your decision to open the door.

Choose to love and to live your life that offers others hope. Honor you word; it's finer than gold. Consider what's best for you and those you love. If you don't, you'll have to accept what life deals out to you. I hope what you'll get to choose is a life fulfillment to love.

"If we choose to see the unseen through your eyes of faith in God, we will have the hope to step forward with grace and strength to walk down the road of your adventurous destiny feeling the freedom in our hearts that we did it. We experienced the

Nature child's Journey!"

Printed in the United States
by Baker & Taylor Publisher Services